Contents

Published and printed in the United States by Merchants Publishing Company
Kalamazoo, Michigan 49001 (All rights reserved) 1976

Publisher's representative for distribution in Canada. Horta Craft Ltd., London, Ontario.

Introduction

Perhaps the best-known flowering plants for indoor uses are those associated with the passing seasons or holidays: the poinsettia, harbinger of Christmas; and daisy-like cinerarias which breathe spring into the wintry air. Yet there is a wide selection of exciting plants which can provide you with a succession of floral color throughout the year. Winter-flowering begonias and bromeliads (e.g. *Billbergia*) are followed closely by the cyclamen, Christ-thorn (*Euphorbia x keysii*) and zygocatus. Springtime brings forth blossom in the goldfish plant (*Columnea*), firecracker flower (*Crossandra*), hydrangea and calceolaria.

As days lengthen more of the gesneriads come into flower: the lipstick vines (*Aeschynanthus*), gloxinia, miniature sinningias, and episcia. Summer is the time for profuse geranium blossom, fuchsias and miniature roses, begonias and impatiens. And as days begin to shorten, flowers appear on the wax plants (*Hoya*), long-lived bromeliads like *Aechmea* and *Neoregelia*, as well as the Persian violet (*Exacum affine*). To complete the year, color continues into winter with the blossoming kalanchoes, poinsettias, the fruits of ornamental peppers and the Christmas cherry.

These are just some of the plants described in this book; plants which you can watch develop and grow, and which add living warmth and color to your home.

Frequently flowering plants serve a two-fold decorative function: they provide the brilliance of color in their season, and, when the flowers have faded, there remain attractive green plants which need not be removed from view.

Care instructions accompany the illustrations throughout this book and the next few pages contain some additional details to help you enjoy long-lived flowering plants.

Conditioning—Help the Plant to Adjust

The change from greenhouse or florist's shop to your home always means an adjustment for the plant, requiring it to become conditioned to its new environment. Home air is drier (lower relative humidity), there is less light available and the temperature is often more uniform and higher than that in which the plant has been growing. The range of flowering plants available for home decoration includes many that are well able to thrive in these different conditions once they have made the adjustment.

You can help the plant adjust in several ways:

—Be sure the soil does not dry out at least for the first week or two, so moisture is always available for the roots to supply the increased needs of leaves and flowers. Cacti and succulents are an exception, however, and should be left dry if purchased during the fall or winter.

—Move the plant to a cooler place at night to reduce water loss in the warm dry air.

—Avoid direct sunlight, even for full sun loving plants; this will keep water losses to a minimum while new roots are developing to sustain the flowers and leaves.

Your new plant may lose a few mature leaves and even some blossoms in its first week or two in the home. This is part of the conditioning process for some plants, and unless losses continue, don't worry. If the plant continues to drop leaves and flowers, some other factor should be suspected; see page 76 for details of plant troubles and how to overcome them.

While each factor is discussed separately, it is the *balance* of light, temperature, water, and nutrition that affects your plant's life. For instance, where temperatures are low, growth slows down or stops and the plant can survive with less light and needs less frequent water and fertilizer applications. Conversely, in a high light position with adequate warmth, growth will accelerate and the plant demands more frequent watering and fertilizing. Thus, when one factor changes, aim to adjust the others accordingly to maintain a balanced environment.

Light

Most flowering plants prefer bright indirect light or partial shade (diffused light), at least while they are in flower. The recommended levels, together with a balance of the remaining environmental factors, aim at prolonging the life of open flowers and at assisting normal development of semi-open blossoms. Tight buds generally open only in brightly lit situations (may even require full sun), with adequate moisture and high relative humidity.

There are a few flowering plants for use in shady locations; these beauties brighten a dull corner or dimly lit room. For example, the bromeliads are able to withstand poor lighting for long periods of time, and the lady's slipper orchid is a shady woodland plant that will not tolerate bright light.

The recommendations on pages 9 through 72 indicate the *minimum* light levels tolerated by plants when they are in flower. Make use of these differences when you select a flowering plant for each location, and enjoy long-lived blossoms and healthy plants. Three basic groups can be identified:

1. *Full sun* and *bright indirect light* loving plants are good in or near sunlit windows, or in places where there is strong reflected light. Flowering plants which enjoy bright indirect light may, however, be burned by the full noonday sun which can quickly dry out the delicate petals.

2. *Partial shade* (diffused light) prevails in an average well-lit position out of direct sunshine, or with a sheer curtain between the plant and sunlight. Plants in this group are best placed 4 to 8 feet from windows; or on a north facing windowsill. These plants also grow well in bright indirect light, though full sun may burn them.

3. *Shade* loving plants grow well with indirect light, in dull corners, or more than 8 feet from a window. These plants can tolerate brighter light, though require conditioning by increasing light intensity in stages over a period of several weeks, rather than all at once.

Temperature

Most flowering plants retain their flowers longer at a temperature cooler than 65°F (18°C). For example, chrysanthemums, kalanchoe, calceolaria, cineraria and azalea are all best with 55-60°F minimum nights (13-16°C). The flowers are of prime importance for many of these plants, and their life will be improved by slightly cooler night temperatures than are found in most living rooms. For the best keeping quality, therefore, move such plants to a cooler place at night.

On the other hand, the African violet, gloxinia, and other gesneriads need average to warm conditions, with night minimum of 60-65°F (16-18°C), for continued life. At cooler temperatures these plants will lose flower buds.

The temperature ranges given with the individual care instructions (pages 9 through 72) are those within which maximum flower life and best growth will be obtained from the plants. But plants will adapt to different environments, and with adequate adjustment of other factors, they can survive at lower (or slightly warmer) temperatures. This is indicated frequently by the statement of tolerance for the individual plant.

1. *Cool* loving plants grow best with day temperatures of 60 to 70°F (16 to 21°C), while nights may be as low as 40 or 45°F (5 or 7°C). Some of these plants are grown out of doors in many parts of the country.

2. *Average* temperature plants need days of 65 to 70°F (18 to 21°C), and up to 75°F (24°C) in the sun; their preferred night minimum range is 50-55°F (10-13°C).

3. *Average to warm* climate plants require days of 70 to 75°F (21 to 24°C) for growth after flowering, and they will not be harmed by as high as 85°F (29°C) in the sun with fresh air. Nights can fall to 60 or 65°F (16 or 18°C), even as low as 55°F (13°C) for some varieties.

Some facts about windows

Sunlight streaming through a window quickly warms up the room. Direct sun heats any surface it falls on, so much that furnishings can be bleached and plants scorched. Delicate plant tissues, especially flowers and plants normally grown in the shade, are most susceptible; but the majority of flowering and foliage plants prefer some protection from full midday sun during summer.

Cool night temperatures outside tend to make the air adjacent to your windows cool too, especially inside single pane windows. In winter the cold air can freeze plants; a temperature of only 40°F (5°C) will chill and damage the warm climate plants and tender flowers. Therefore, on winter nights bring plants away from the windows. Aim to avoid temperature fluctuations, for even though most plants thrive when nights are from 10 to 15°F cooler than days (a drop of 6 to 8°C), a rapid change of 30-40°F (16-22°C) in either direction can kill.

Humidity

A number of flowering plants need relatively humid air for the best development; some will lose buds if humidity is too low. However, this requirement does not make them difficult to grow. Your well-lighted kitchen and bathroom naturally provide the increased humidity for such plants. In other rooms, raise the humidity around the plants by using them in groups, or by placing them on wet gravel or sand.

Watering

How often to water flowering plants

The water balance of plants in full flower is usually a lot more critical than that for foliage plants. Many flowers are more tender than the leaves of the same plants, and the petals lose water very rapidly; they are the first tissues to suffer from a water deficit. If it is left to dry even just once, the calceolaria or cineraria will suffer irreversible damage even though part of the plant recovers after the soil is remoistened.

Most flowering plants, therefore, need to have their soil kept uniformly moist though not wet while they are in flower. Variations on how frequently to water after flowering are noted in the individual sections. You can tell when the plant needs water by the feel or look of its soil; the weight of the pot is another indicator. The rate at which that plant uses and loses water depends on variety, growth rate, temperature, light, and relative humidity. Let the plant itself be your guide to watering at all times of the year; plants in flower tend to need more frequent watering than others, even in the same room.

When the soil surface is dark and damp to the touch, the whole root ball is probably moist—as it should be if you've just watered it. While it dries out, the soil surface color gets lighter though it will continue to feel moist for some time. The surface generally dries before soil further down in the container, so let the top 'feel' of soil be your indicator and the entire root ball will not dry out.

In care instructions for plants, three different watering requirements are noted:

1. There are some plants that should not be allowed to dry, ever. They can be watered again when the soil surface starts drying, before it gets powder-dry.

2. Most plants for indoor use need to be kept uniformly moist but not wet. The soil surface can be allowed to dry more than those in the first group, and you won't do any harm if the plants sometimes dry out entirely for brief periods. But frequent drying out will cause damage, resulting in leaf losses.

3. Plants such as cacti and succulents thrive when their soil is allowed to dry out between waterings.

How much water to give plants

No matter how often or rarely you water the plant, be sure each time that the whole root ball (all the soil) is thoroughly moistened; and that the excess water can drain out of the container if possible.

A thorough watering followed by a period of time to allow the soil at least to start drying, permits air to be drawn into the root ball. Plant roots need oxygen for life and growth, and if they are constantly saturated by water 'little and often' they will soon die.

Is tap water OK?

Generally yes, though water from the cold tap may be too cold for the plants. It is best to use water at room temperature; that is, above 60°F, for indoor plants. Either add a little warm water (don't cook the plants!) or leave it to stand overnight so the water warms to room temperature.

Fluorides can be harmful to some plants though few flowering plants are affected. Specific indoor plants which show damage are *Dracaena, Cordyline,* and *Chlorophytum;* also *Maranta* (Prayer Plant), *Calathea,* and *Agave.* Over a period of time, added fluorides cause brown spots and/or leaf tip burn on the sensitive ones.

The quantity of fluoride normally added to municipal water supplies is sufficient to harm these plants. Perlite, a soil additive often used to help soil aeration, also contains potentially harmful amounts of fluoride.

To overcome or avoid fluoride damage:

1. Avoid the use of fluoridated water. Other sources are snow, rain, well or spring-water (this can be checked by your local or state testing center for mineral content), and dehumidifier-water.

2. Adjust the pH of your potting soil to 6.0-6.5 or slightly higher; in this range the fluorides are relatively harmless to plants. Repot in soil containing dolomite limestone to raise pH, replacing as much soil as possible in the plant's root ball.

3. Avoid the use of superphosphate in your potting mix; superphosphate contains a high level of fluoride.

Chlorine in tap water does not usually harm plants, and if you allow the water to stand in an open container for 12 to 24 hours, most of the chlorine will escape. However, the one exception to the relative harmlessness of chlorine is in misting or spraying fern fronds; as this water evaporates, any chlorine in it will cause browning of the delicate fronds.

Water-softener water will not harm your plants, provided the softening equipment is functioning correctly. This water still contains chemicals, though the lime has been replaced with more soluble compounds.

Fertilization

Flowering plants which are enjoyed for a season of only a few weeks will not require any additional fertilizer while they are in flower. Others, whose growth continues even while they bear blossoms, will need regular fertilizer applications. See Pages 9 through 72 for instructions on the flowering plants contained in this book.

Even if your new flowering plant is growing vigorously, it is wise to wait a month while it adjusts to its new environment, before adding fertilizer. Likewise, a newly potted plant needs time in which to grow new roots to absorb the fertilizer you'll be applying. And after dormancy, it is best to wait until the first leaves are fully expanded before resuming fertilizer applications.

It is often easier to feed a number of plants at the same time, and the schedules can be combined; for a general practice, apply fertilizer to most long-term indoor plants every 1-2 months while growth is rapid, and once or twice only during the winter months. Alternatively, apply the plant food more frequently in a dilute form; this accomodates plants which would be injured by full strength fertilizer. 'Half the recommended strength' means using only half as much fertilizer per plant or in solution.

Short term or annual plants grow very quickly and need fertilizing every two or three weeks during their short season. Some flowering plants, like azalea, should not be fertilized at all while they are in flower.

Type of fertilizer

Any prepared mixture for the type of plants you have is fine; for most house plants, an N-P-K analysis ratio that is close to 1-2-1 will give balanced growth. African Violets are best with a mix containing more nitrogen (N); and there are other formulations available for the acid-loving plants like Azalea and Gardenia. For annuals and other garden plants growing in containers, an outdoor fertilizer is fine.

Soluble compounds are easy to apply and show quicker results than solids or slow release pellets. Simply apply the fertilizer solution in place of water when you would normally be watering the plants. However, be sure the soil is slightly damp when you fertilize; never feed plants with dry soil, because roots will be damaged by the chemicals you add unless they are diluted further by soil moisture.

Use all fertilizers at or weaker than the recommended strength of dilution, never stronger. Newly rooted cuttings, seedlings, and young plants will benefit from weaker solutions to avoid damage to the soft young roots.

Soluble Salts—Leaching Flowering Plants

When you fertilize your plants, you add chemicals to the soil; water contains chemicals too, so even when you water them, you are adding to the soluble salt content of the soil. The growing plant does not, nor does it need to, absorb all of these soluble chemicals. They accumulate in the soil. High concentrations will damage the plant, causing loss of roots and subsequent foliage loss, reduced size of new growth, wilting even while the soil is moist, and collapse of the whole plant. Soluble salt problems are less likely to occur with short term flowering plants, or with those that need a rest period plus repotting in new soil each year.

Good watering practices help to keep the soluble salt build-up to a minimum, if the excess water (really a solution) is discarded every time you water. But with regular fertilization and watering, the accumulated soluble salts should be washed out of the soil by leaching at intervals of 2-3 months.

TO LEACH; immerse the container in a bowl of water to saturate the root ball and all the soil; after about 30 minutes, or when bubbles stop rising, remove and allow it to drain. Containers with no drainage holes should be tilted to permit the drainage solution to run out over the edge. Repeat this procedure one or more times with clean water.

Repotting

Type of soil
Information accompanying the plant illustrations in this book includes a note about the type of soil preferred by each group of plants. It is important for many flowering plants that the soil retain sufficient moisture, so you don't have to water them constantly.

Generally, the same basic mix can be used for all indoor plants: this consists of equal parts (by volume) sterilized soil, peatmoss, and sharp sand. Or use a mix containing two parts peatmoss and one part sharp sand. For reasons of weight, the sand portion can be replaced with perlite. This basic mix is then varied to come closer to the content and texture of the soil in which your plant is already growing; or added to more peatmoss as needed for a more humusy combination.

To sterilize your own soil, first moisten it, and then heat it in a covered (not sealed) fireproof dish in the oven. Its temperature should reach 160-180°F (70-82°C) (use a meat thermometer if you have one), and remain there for about 25 minutes. After cooling, add the peatmoss, sand, and any other additions you require.

Containers and drainage
Plant containers are as varied as the plants they hold: clay, ceramic, glass, plastic or wood pots or bowls, for single specimens or for whole groups of plants together. The container markedly affects how often your plant will need water; for example, the water loss through the sides of a porous clay pot is about three times that from a plastic pot (most of the loss from plastic pots is from the soil surface, not through the pot sides). When you have two specimens of the same variety of plant, side by side with one in plastic and the other in clay, you can quickly see the difference.

A container with drainage holes in its base makes watering easy because you can see when all the soil has been moistened. The excess drains out, so there is no danger of waterlogging which will soon kill the plant's roots. With some experience, though, watering plants in watertight containers can be just as successful and can result in plants which are every bit as healthy as those in pots with drainage holes.

Clay, plastic, wood, metal, and pottery containers can be planted just like any flower pot, with a piece of broken pot or pebbles at the bottom so the drainage hole doesn't become clogged with soil or the soil components wash out of the pot. For containers without drainage holes, a layer of coarse material under the soil acts as a buffer against overwatering, so roots are not continually in the accumulated water.

Mesh containers for hanging plants should be lined with plastic, or with sheet or sphagnum moss. The plastic will prevent dripping, though you should punch a few holes at the bottom to help drainage.

Acknowledgements

Copy for this book was prepared by M. Jane Coleman, Ph.D., technical writer; and by Laura L. Williams, M.Sc., horticultural specialist, both of Merchants Publishing Company.

The photographs are from Merchants' comprehensive library of horticultural subjects; a collection of over 14,000 pictures compiled by horticultural photographers John Pike and the late Willard Kalina.

We thank the following companies and individuals for their kind cooperation in providing assistance, materials and some additional photographs for *Flowering Plants for Modern Living:*

Abbey Garden, Carpinteria, California; California Color, Watsonville, California; B. L. Cobia, Inc., Winter Garden, Florida; Davids & Royston Bulb Co. Inc., Gardena, California; Peter De Groot, De Groot, Inc., Coloma, Michigan; Green Thumb Products, Apopka, Florida; Mr. & Mrs. Robert Hansen, Watsonville, California; Hines Wholesale Nurseries, Santa Ana, California; Michigan State University Horticulture Greenhouses, East Lansing, Michigan; Modesta Floral, Grand Rapids, Michigan; Nurserymens Exchange, San Francisco, California; Plants Galore, Kalamazoo, Michigan; Presidio Nurseries Inc., San Diego, California; Riverside Greenhouses, Kalamazoo, Michigan; Rogers' Mesa Del Mar Garden Center, Newport Beach, California; Romence Garden Center, Kalamazoo, Michigan; Select Nurseries Inc., Brea, California; Earl J. Small Growers, Inc., Pinellas Park, Florida; Bonnie E. Stewart, Kalamazoo, Michigan; Jarmila Tesar, Kalamazoo, Michigan; Mr. & Mrs. Glen Thomas, Newport Beach, California; VanderSalm Greenhouses, Kalamazoo, Michigan; Weber Bros. Greenhouses, Inc., Oak Park, Michigan; Dr. Louis Wilson, Michigan State University, East Lansing, Michigan.

Flowering Plants for Modern Living contains a broad range of flowering plants grown for indoor decoration. There are over 100 full color photographs of subjects used both as seasonal decoration and year round specimens valued both for foliage and flowers.

The pictures are accompanied by individual care instructions for each genus or plant group; these details include the light, temperature, watering, fertilization and soil needs, some suggested uses for the plants, and information about reflowering. Introductory sections deal with the general care of plants in terms of their environmental needs, and factors which influence flowering response. There are also indexes of common and botanical names of the flowering plants illustrated in this book, and charts for disorders, pests and diseases of indoor plants.

WEEPING CHINESE LANTERN
Aubutilon megapotamicum variegatum
Graceful, drooping branches with variegated leaves and pendant "lanterns" of red and sunny yellow.

Abutilon

Caring For Your Abutilon

Temperature: Average climate; minimum at night 50-55°F (10-13°C).

Light: Bright indirect light to full sun.

Watering: Keep soil moist, not wet.

Fertilize: Monthly in spring and summer. Every 2-3 months in fall and winter or when not growing rapidly.

Soil: Any general houseplant mix or soil that permits good drainage.

Uses: Chinese lantern for hanging baskets or placed on plant stands or pedestals. Flowering maple as a shrubby specimen in plant groupings, or displayed singly. Both excellent plants for summer color on balcony or patio.

After flowering: Continue to water and fertilize regularly while growing actively, decreasing watering and fertilization as growth slows in winter. Prune after flowering to encourage bushiness. Abutilons bloom at any time of year with adequate light.

SPOTTED FLOWERING MAPLE
Abutilon striatum thompsonii
Shrubby plant with maple-shaped leaves splattered cream and yellow. The flowers resemble those of hollyhock.

9

Chenille Plant

Acalypha hispida

Pendulous, tassel-like blossoms to 12 inches (30 cm) hang from each branch in summer. Becomes a large shrub with age.

Caring For Your Chenille Plant

Temperature: Average to warm climate; minimum at night 55-60°F (13-16°C).

Light: Partial shade to full sun.

Watering: Keep soil evenly moist but not wet.

Fertilize: Monthly in spring and summer. Every 2 months through fall and winter.

Soil: Any general house plant mix or soil that permits good drainage.

Uses: Small plants for color accents when in flower. Mature specimens in floor groupings of indoor plants or outdoors in summer. Light pruning after blooming will encourage fullness.

Shrimp Plant

Beloperone guttata

Continuous flowering houseplant with rusty-red, shingled bracts resembling the tail of a shrimp.

Caring For Your Shrimp Plant

Temperature: Average climate; minimum at night 50-55°F (10-13°C). Tolerates as low as 40°F (5°C) for short periods.

Light: Bright indirect light or full sun.

Watering: Soil may dry out between waterings.

Fertilize: Every month.

Soil: Any general houseplant mix or soil that permits good drainage.

Uses: Small accent plant when young. Spindly plants should be pruned frequently to encourage branching and fullness before blooming.

Acanthus Family

FIRECRACKER FLOWER
Crossandra infundibuliformis

Glossy leaves and clusters of creamy tangerine blooms characterize this tropical plant. Blossoms continually with sufficient light. **(Top)**

ZEBRA PLANT
Aphelandra squarrosa

Striking foliage or flowering plant blooming naturally in summer and fall. Frequently blossoms upon becoming pot bound. **(Center)**

Care Instructions

Temperature: Average to warm climate; minimum at night 55-60°F (13-16°C).

Light: Bright indirect light or partial shade. Gold Hops prefers humid air.

Watering: Keep soil evenly moist. Drying of soil will result in lower leaf drop on Zebra Plants.

Soil: Add peat moss to an equal volume of house plant mix for Firecracker Flower and Zebra Plants. Gold Hops will grow well in any general houseplant mix or soil that permits good drainage.

Uses: Flowering specimen or foliage plants, adding colorful accents to plant groups when in flower.

GOLD HOPS
Pachystachys lutea

Lemon yellow bracts surround white, 2 lipped flowers in late summer. **(Bottom)**

11

Flamingo Plant

Jacobinia carnea

Summer blooming house or patio plant with arching flowers produced above the deep green leaves. Pinch stem tips to encourage bushiness.

Caring For Your Flamingo Plant

Temperature: Average to warm climate, mimumum at night 60-65°F (16-18°C). Tolerates as low as 40°F (5°C) for short periods.

Light: Partial shade or bright diffused light.

Watering: Keep soil evenly moist but not wet.

Fertilize: Monthly when not in flower.

Soil: Any general house plant mix or soil that permits good drainage.

Uses: Remove flower heads as they fade and begin regular fertilization. Small plants are displayed effectively on shelf or table; larger ones as floor specimens. Patio plant in sheltered location during summer.

Black-eyed Susan Vine *Thunbergia alata*

Vining bloomer with 1½" (3-4 cm) diameter blooms scattered liberally throughout the triangular leaves. Shows to best advantage if provided with trellis type support for the twining stems.

Caring For Your Black-eyed Susan Vine

Temperature: Average climate, minimum at night 50-60°F (10-16°C). Tolerates as low as 40°F (5°C) for long periods, making little or no new growth.

Light: Bright indirect light or full sun.

Watering: Keep soil evenly moist but not wet.

Fertilize: Every 2-4 weeks while growing rapidly.

Soil: Any general house plant mix or soil that permits good drainage.

Uses: Commonly grown from seed for use as a summer annual on porch or patio. Flowering indoor plant in brightly lit areas, adapted well to hanging basket culture.

12

Amaryllis *Hippeastrum hybrid*

Tropical bulb producing large, lily-type flowers on a 1-2 foot (30-60 cm) stalk. Can be reflowered successfully for years.

Caring For Your Amaryllis

Temperature: Average to warm climate, minimum at night 50-55°F (10-13°C).

Light: Bright diffused light or full sun.

Watering: Keep soil evenly moist but not wet during growing and flowering periods.

Fertilize: Monthly during growing and flowering.

Soil: Any general house plant mix or soil that permits good drainage.

Uses: Striking specimen plant for table or windowsill display.

After flowering: Remove blossoms as they fade and continue watering regularly throughout spring and summer. Applying fertilizer once monthly during this period will help increase the vigor of the bulb and promote flowering the following year. The Amaryllis leaves will begin to turn yellow and dry in late summer as the bulb enters its dormant period. Reduce watering frequency at this time and do not fertilize. The soil should be allowed to dry out thoroughly. The bulb will remain dormant throughout the fall and winter, and may be reflowered in late winter. To reflower, resume watering and fertilizing the dormant bulb. The bulb will begin to grow within 2 weeks and blooms will appear in 4-6 weeks.

Anthurium *Anthurium andraeanum*

Long-lasting, heart-shaped flowers appear continuously throughout the year.

Caring For Your Anthurium

Temperature: Average to warm; minimum at night 65°F (18°C).

Light: Indirect sunlight or partial shade. Prefers humid air.

Watering: Keep soil evenly moist but not wet.

Fertilize: Every month.

Soil: Add peat moss to an equal volume of general houseplant mix for a humusy and well drained combination.

Uses: Continuous flowering specimen plant for floor or table display.

14

Spathiphyllum

MINIATURE SPATHIPHYLLUM ▸
Spathiphyllum floribundum

Dwarf type Spathiphyllum with matte green leaves and dependably continuous flowers with moderate light. Extremely drought sensitive.

Caring For Your Spathiphyllum

Temperature: Average to warm climate; minimum at night 60-65°F (16-18°C). Tolerates as low as 55°F (13°C) for short periods.

Light: Bright indirect light for best flowering. Tolerates full shade but flowering decreases.

Watering: Never allow soil to dry out, though do not saturate it.

Fertilize: Every 2 months.

Soil: Any general house plant mix or soil that permits good drainage.

Uses: Foliage or flowering plants. Dwarf Spathiphyllum on table or shelf. Spathiphyllum 'Clevelandii' as a floor specimen.

PEACE LILY ▸
Spathiphyllum 'Clevelandii'

Open growing foliage or flowering houseplant with handsome white flowers year round. 12-30 inches (30-75 cm) tall.

Azalea *Rhododendron hybrid*

Well-known flowering woody shrubs with blossoms lasting for a 1-2 month period.

Caring For Your Azalea

Temperature: Average to cool climate, minimum at night 50-60°F (10-16°C).

Light: Bright indirect light; avoid full sun to prevent blossom burn.

Watering: Never let soil dry out, though do not saturate it or allow the pot to stand in water.

Fertilizer: None needed while Azalea is flowering.

Soil: An acid mix of peatmoss with half as much or an equal volume of general house plant soil.

Uses: Colorful specimen plant to brighten any room.

After flowering: Water regularly to maintain active growth; fertilize every 2-4 weeks. Give a shaded position outdoors when spring frost danger is past. Trim to shape by mid-July. Flower buds form in summer and fall. When nights become cooler, reduce watering frequency and fertilize every 4-6 weeks. Bring Azalea indoors before frost, but maintain it in a cool room (45-50°F, 7-10°C) for 1-2 months until flower color shows.

Coral Berry Ardisia crispa

Thickened, shiny leaves with slightly fluted edges cover this shrubby tropical plant. Fragrant white or red blossoms give way to clusters of red berries which adorn the plant for a long time — several months to a year.

Caring For Your Coral Berry

Temperature: Average to cool climate, minimum at night 45-50°F (7-10°C).

Light: Partial shade or bright indirect light.

Watering: Keep soil uniformly moist but not wet.

Fertilize: Every 1-2 months.

Soil: Any general house plant mix or soil that permits good drainage.

Uses: Specimen for table or shelf. Attractive foliage persists year round.

After flowering: Fruits may persist for a full year. If new growth is slow in fall and winter, allow soil to dry slightly between waterings and reduce fertilizer applications. In spring, prune to shape as desired, and increase water and fertilizer rates as new growth is made. Coral Berry produces fragrant white or red flowers in summer; fruit develop and are fully colored by midwinter.

18

Troutleaf Begonia *Begonia 'Medora'*

Outstanding fibrous-rooted begonia. Deep green leaves are lightly sprinkled with silver, contrasting with the graceful pink flower clusters. This cane-stemmed begonia makes an excellent indoor plant, and will grow to a full, bushy specimen, several feet tall.

Caring For Your Fibrous-rooted Begonia: See Page 20.

Fuchsia Begonia *Begonia fuchsioides floribunda*

Familiar flowering begonia for indoors, with its profusion of small blossoms. A fibrous-rooted variety.

Caring For Your Fibrous Begonia

Temperature: Average climate, minimum at night 55-60°F (13-16°C).

Light: Bright indirect light or partial shade.

Watering: Keep soil uniformly moist but not wet.

Fertilize: Every month while growing vigorously.

Soil: Any general house plant mix or soil that permits good drainage.

Uses: Indoor flowering plant for brightly lighted areas, specimen plant for table, shelf, or hanging basket. Flowers continuously with adequate light: place in east or north unshaded window during winter.

Mapleleaf Begonia *Begonia* x *'Cleopatra'*

Delightful rhizomatous begonia with interesting foliage as well as charmingly delicate flower clusters.

Caring For Your Rhizomatous Begonia

Temperature: Average to warm climate, minimum at night 60-65°F (16-18°C).

Light: Partial shade or bright indirect light.

Watering: Keep soil uniformly moist but not wet.

Fertilize: Apply at half the recommended strength every month.

Soil: Add peatmoss to an equal volume of general house plant mix for a humusy and well drained combination.

Uses: Small specimen for table, shelf or windowsill.

After flowering: Continue to water and fertilize regularly while growth is active. Leaves may die back or growth slow down in winter; do not fertilize until new foliage shows, and reduce watering frequency while plant is resting. Rhizomatous Begonia flowers form with adequate light, during the longer days of spring and summer.

VARIEGATED WAX BEGONIA
Begonia semperflorens 'Charm'

Rounded to oval leaves and continual flowering are typical of the wax begonias. Variegated types add interest through their bright markings in white and yellow on the fresh green foliage.

Caring For Your Wax Begonia

Temperature: Average to cool climate, minimum at night 50-55°F (10-13°C).

Light: Bright diffused sunlight, full sun in winter. Shade outdoors. Best in cooler climates.

Watering: Soil may dry slightly between waterings.

Fertilize: Every month.

Soil: Add peatmoss to an equal volume of general house plant mix for a humusy and well drained combination.

Uses: Small specimen plants, adding color to mixed plant groups. In containers for porch and patio, hanging baskets or summer bedding plant. Flowers continuously with adequate light.

WAX BEGONIA
Begonia semperflorens

The delicate, sprightly flowers of wax begonias are handsome and long lasting. Lots of sun will ensure the continued production of cheerful blossoms.

22

Flattened underground tubers sprout readily in late winter, to produce lavish fresh green foliage and blossoms. Other forms include those with flowers shaped like camellias and carnations, on pendulous or upright plants.

Tuberous Begonias *Begonia tuberhybrida*

Caring For Your Tuberous Begonias

Temperature: Average to cool climate, minimum at night 50-55°F (10-13°C).

Light: Bright diffused sunlight. Shade outdoors. Best in cooler climates.

Watering: Keep soil moist but not wet.

Fertilize: Every month while growing.

Soil: Add peatmoss to an equal volume of general house plant mix for a humusy and well drained combination.

Uses: Specimen plants or in mixed plant groups. In containers for porch and patio. Hanging baskets (pendulous types). Summer bedding plants for shaded areas.

After flowering: Reduce watering frequency and stop fertilizing as leaves die back. Lift tubers and store in a frost-free, dry, dark place; or leave tubers in dry soil for storage. In late winter, replant in fresh soil and water well, placing in bright light to encourage strong new growth. Keep soil moist.

Once the first leaves are full expanded, resume monthly fertilizer applications. Begonia tubers can be planted directly outdoors; or, start plants inside and move out when all frost danger is past and nights remain above 40°F (5°C).

The Bromeliads

◀ **SILVER VASE**
Aechmea fasciata

Aechmeas are among the most beautiful of all Bromeliads for indoor decoration. Large, colorful blooms rise high above the vase-shaped rosette of leaves. Long lasting flowers are followed by colorful berries which persist for many months.

VASE PLANT
Aechmea calyculata
(Below)
▼

Aechmea

Caring For Your Aechmea

Temperature: Average to warm climate, minimum at night 60-65°F (16-18°C). Tolerates as low as 40° (5°) for extended periods, though makes little or no new growth.

Light: Partial shade or bright indirect light. Also tolerates shade.

Watering: Soil may dry out between waterings. Keep water in central cup formed by the leafy rosette.

Fertilize: Every 1-2 months, applied to the soil. Or fill the cup with half-strength dilution of fertilizer every month.

Soil: Add peatmoss to an equal volume of general house plant mix for a humusy and well drained combination.

Uses: Superb specimen plant with flowers lasting several months. Grow as a foliage plant between flowerings.

Reflowering Your Bromeliad: See page 27.

Queen's Tears *Billbergia nutans*

Pendulous flower clusters on long pink stems make this a colorful and graceful item. Its durable nature and tolerance of neglect make it doubly valuable.

Caring For Your Queen's Tears

Temperature: Average climate, minimum at night 55-60°F (13-16°C). Tolerates as cool as 40°F (5°C).

Light: Partial shade or bright indirect light. Also tolerates shade.

Watering: Soil may dry out between waterings.

Fertilize: Every 1-2 months.

Soil: Add peatmoss to an equal volume of general house plant mix for a humusy and well drained combination.

Uses: Specimen plant with long flowering period.

Reflowering Your Bromeliad: See page 27.

ORANGE STAR
Guzmania lingulata 'Minor'

Small Bromeliad with showy orange bracts at center, preceding the cluster of white blossoms which remain close to the star-like bract rosette.

Guzmania and Neoregelia

Caring For Your Guzmania and Neoregelia

Temperature: Average to warm, night minimum 60-65°F (16-18°C). Tolerates 45°F (7°C) for short periods.

Light: Partial shade or bright diffused light. Guzmania prefers humid air, while Neoregelia tolerates drier indoor conditions.

Watering: Keep soil moist but not wet. Maintain water in central cup.

Fertilize: Every 1-2 months, applied to the soil. Or fill the cup with half-strength dilution of fertilizer every month.

Soil: Add peatmoss to an equal volume of general house plant mix.

Uses: Specimen plants for colorful decoration during the long flowering period.

Reflowering Your Bromeliad:
See Page 27.

BLUSHING BROMELIAD
Neoregelia carolinae

An unusual Bromeliad with very flat rosette. Cup and center leaves deep crimson; flowers are borne deep within the cup.

26

Flaming Sword

Vriesia splendens 'Major'
Dusty green leaves are banded with broad stripes of subtle purple. The flattened orange bracts of the flower spike protect yellow flowers.

Caring For Your Flaming Sword

Temperature: Average to warm climate, minimum at night 60-65°F (16-18°C). Tolerates as low as 45°F (7°C) for short periods.

Light: Partial shade or bright diffused light. Prefers humid air.

Watering: Soil may dry out between waterings. Keep water in central cup formed by the leafy rosette.

Fertilize: Every 1-2 months, applied to the soil. Or fill the cup with half-strength dilution of fertilizer every month.

Soil: Add peatmoss to an equal volume of general house plant mix for a humusy and well drained combination.

Uses: Fine decorator specimen for the 3-6 month flowering period. Grow as a foliage plant between flowerings.

Reflowering Your Bromeliad: After flowering, Bromeliads produce side shoots (offsets), which may be removed while young and rooted for additional plants. Most bromeliads will flower naturally when they reach maturity; they can also be made to flower by supplying the substances which begin bud formation: for example, enclose the entire plant (with its cup empty of water to prevent excessive humidity buildup) in a plastic bag together with a ripe apple. The apple gives off ethylene gas which stimulates flowering in Bromeliads. Leave plant and the apple in the plastic bag for 7-10 days; flowers will appear in 1-2 months.

Cactus

RAINBOW CACTUS ⌃
*Echinocereus pectinatus
v. neomexicanus*

CHIN CACTI ⌃ *Gymnocalycium quehlianum* (Top)
Gymnocalycium baldianum (Lower left and right)

Caring For Your Cacti

Temperature: Average climate, minimum at night 55°F (13°C) in spring and summer. Cooler in fall and winter (45-55°F, 7-13°C).

Light: Full sun, but beware of burning new cacti with excess sun when first acquired.

Watering: Keep soil slightly moist in spring and summer. In winter, allow to dry out completely between light waterings.

Fertilizer: Every 5-8 weeks in spring and summer with low nitrogen fertilizer.

Soil: A combination of equal parts of a general house plant mix and sharp sand. Avoid excess peat moss.

Uses: Specimen plants or use in cacti and succulent dish gardens. Outdoors on patio or balcony in summer.

After flowering: Continue to water and fertilize regularly while growth is active in spring and summer. Many cacti flower only after a rest period in winter. In fall, place cacti in a cool, well lit location (45-55°F, 7-13°C); a south window is best. Turn plants weekly so all sides receive direct sun. Water infrequently and do not fertilize. Flower buds form in spring; increase water and resume fertilization.

◀ **PIN-CUSHION**
Mammillaria hybrid

28

◀ **DARK FLORIDA CHRIST-THORN**
Euphorbia x keysii

PINK FLORIDA CHRIST-THORN
Euphorbia x. 'Flamingo'
(Below) ▼

Crown of Thorns

Succulent, spiny plants with close-set leaves and brilliantly colored flower bracts. Sturdy branches grow to 10-18 inches long (25-45 cm).

Caring For Your Crown of Thorns

Temperature: Average to warm climate, minimum at night 60-65°F (16-18°C).

Light: Full sun or bright indirect light.

Watering: Keep soil uniformly moist but not wet.

Fertilize: Every 4-6 months.

Soil: Any general house plant mix or soil that permits good drainage.

Uses: Specimen for table, shelf, windowsill. Add to plant groups, dish gardens. Flowers continuously, particularly in winter and spring. Needs adequate light for flowering and leaf maintenance.

Christmas Cactus Zygocactus truncatus

Branching succulent composed of many 'leaves' or segments with toothed edges. Flowers for several weeks.

Caring For Your Christmas Cactus

Temperature: Average to warm climate, minimum at night 62-65°F (17-18°C).

Light: Bright diffused light in spring and summer, full sun in fall and winter.

Watering: Keep soil uniformly moist but not wet.

Fertilize: Every 2-4 weeks while growing vigorously.

Soil: Add peatmoss to an equal volume of general house plant mix for a humusy and well drained combination.

Uses: Specimen plant for table, shelf, windowsill, hanging baskets.

After flowering: Water and fertilize regularly through spring and summer, while plant is growing. For bud formation, Christmas Cactus requires drier, cooler conditions, plus the shorter days of fall. If kept indoors, try to avoid any extension of natural days by the use of electric lights: keep the plant in a room not used during the evening hours. In fall, reduce watering frequency and keep plant cooler (night minimum 55-60°F, 13-16°C). Increase water when buds appear; fertilize with half-strength dilution every 2 weeks until flowers are open, then resume normal fertilization practice.

30

Coleus *Coleus blumei*

Dependable favorites valued primarily for outstanding foliage colors of red, orange, yellow and green. Flowers are tiny, pale lavender blossoms in spikes at shoot tips.

Caring For Your Coleus

Temperature: Average to warm climate, minimum at night 60-65°F (16-18°C).

Light: Full sun or bright indirect light.

Watering: Keep soil moist but not wet.

Fertilize: Apply at half the recommended rate every month.

Soil: Any general house plant mix or soil that permits good drainage.

Uses: Decorator item with color accent foliage for windowsill, shelf, table. Pinch tips to retain bushy habit.

Glory Bower *Clerodendrum thomsonae*

Semi-vining patio and indoor plant. Deep green, shiny leaves on stems which can climb to 6-10 feet. Prune to maintain shorter, bushy habit.

Caring For Your Glory Bower

Temperature: Average to warm climate, minimum at night 60-65°F (16-18°C).

Light: Partial shade or bright indirect sunlight.

Watering: Keep soil moist but not wet.

Fertilize: Every 2-4 weeks while growing vigorously.

Soil: Any general house plant mix or soil that permits good drainage.

Uses: Hanging basket or trailing, climbing plant.

After flowering: Continue to water and fertilize regularly while growth is active. Reduce watering frequency in late fall, as growth slows, stop fertilizing and maintain Clerodendrum in a cooler room (50-60°F, 10-16°C) until early spring. Resume regular watering and fertilization as new growth starts. With adequate warmth, Glory Bower will continue flowering from spring into winter.

31

Pocketbook Plant *Calceolaria herbeohybrida*

Pouch or slipper-shaped flowers in many brilliant and decorated hues, to brighten any spring.

Caring For Your Calceolaria

Temperature: Cool climate, minimum at night 40-45°F (5-7°C) for best keeping quality.

Light: Bright indirect light, avoid direct sun.

Watering: Soil may dry out between thorough waterings, though do not let foliage wilt.

Fertilize: None needed while Calceolaria is in flower.

Soil: Any general house plant mix or soil that permits good drainage.

Uses: Colorful decorator item for seasonal display.

After flowering: Leaves die back rapidly to soil level. Calceolaria is a tender perennial usually grown as an annual and discarded after flowering.

Cineraria *Senecio cruentus*

Profusely blooming plant for cool locations. Clusters of daisy-like flowers in a rainbow of hues often completely cover foliage.

Caring For Your Cineraria

Temperature: Cool climate, minimum at night 40-45°F (5-7°C). Best where days do not exceed 68°F (20°C).

Light: Bright diffused light or partial shade; avoid direct sun.

Watering: Keep soil uniformly moist but not wet; never allow soil to dry out completely.

Fertilizer: None needed while your Cineraria is flowering.

Soil: Any general house plant mix or soil that permits good drainage.

Uses: Bright decorator item for accent, centerpiece, massed display.

After Flowering: Leaves die back rapidly to soil level. Cineraria is a tender perennial usually grown as an annual and discarded after flowering.

From Seed: Sow from June through early September in a cool greenhouse (night minimum 45-50° F, 7-10° C) for late winter and spring flowers. Transplant to final pots very early. Once established, fertilize every 2-3 weeks.

33

Ornamental Peppers

RED CLUSTER PEPPER
Capsicum annuum "Fiesta"

Upright, slim peppers change color from yellow to orange to red, contrasting with the deep green foliage. The peppers are edible, but extremely hot.

Caring For Your Ornamental Pepper

Temperature: Average to warm climate minimum at night 60-65°F (16-18°C).

Light: Bright diffused light or full sun.

Watering: Keep soil uniformly moist but not wet.

Fertilizer: None needed once your Ornamental Pepper has flowered and set fruit.

Soil: Any general house plant mix or soil that permits good drainage.

Uses: Cheerful accent and conversation piece for low table, windowsill. Edible hot peppers for seasoning foods. Discard Ornamental Peppers when fruits lose their decorative appeal and leaves are shed.

From Seed: In greenhouse conditions, night minimum 55-60°F (13-16°C). Sow right into pots in January and February; pinch established plants until mid-July to encourage bushiness. Fertilize every month until flowering. Seed sown in June, 3 per pot, unpinched, also will bear fruit for Christmas.

CHRISTMAS CANDLE
Capsicum annuum conoides

Conical fruits follow star-shaped white flowers at shoot-tips of this compact plant. Peppers last several weeks, ripening to an orange-red color.

Christmas Cherry *Solanum pseudo-capsicum*

Also well-known as Jerusalem Cherry, Cleveland Cherry. Excellent indoor plant that can be kept year after year. Tiny white flowers in summer, followed by long lasting orange cherry-like fruits. Fruits are inedible and may harm some individuals.

Caring For Your Christmas Cherry

Temperature: Average climate, minimum at night 50-55° F (10-13°C).

Light: Bright indirect light or full sun.

Watering: Soil may become partially dry between waterings.

Fertilize: Every month.

Soil: Any general house plant mix or soil that permits good drainage.

Uses: Colorful fruits add decorative accent throughout the winter months. Place on brightly lighted table, windowsill.

To grow on: After fruits and leaves have been shed, cut stems back 2-3". Repot and plunge outdoors, fertilize monthly, and pinch vigorously growing stem tips until late June to encourage branching and to shape as desired. Flowers in summer.

From Seed: Sow in February and March, transplant to pots and finish as above.

35

Classic flowering houseplants with blooms that last several weeks. Bright indirect light, cool nights and evenly moist soil will extend flower life.

Caring For Your Pot Chrysanthemum

Temperature: Average to cool climate, minimum at night 50-60°F (10-16°C).

Light: Bright indirect light; shade from direct sun to prevent burning.

Watering: Keep soil uniformly moist but not wet.

Fertilizer: None needed while your pot chrysanthemum is in flower.

Soil: Any general house plant mix or soil that permits good drainage.

Pot Chrysanthemum *Chrysanthemum morifolium*

Uses: Any well lighted position in the house or office. Single or massed displays. Use on porch or patio during the warmer months.

After flowering: Gradually reduce watering frequency as leaves die down. In winter maintain the resting plant in a cool dark place, keeping soil barely damp until spring.

When plant can be moved out of doors, cut stems back to 2-4" from soil and plunge pot or plant in sunny place. Water thoroughly. When new growth starts, fertilize every two weeks. Prune and pinch to shape through early summer. Cuttings from new growth can make new plants.

Chrysanthemums flower naturally as days become shorter (longer nights) in late summer to fall. Tender greenhouse varieties may not survive early frosts or winter freezes: lift pots and place in bright position indoors.

Pot chrysanthemum varieties often grow much taller in home conditions than when grown in a commercial greenhouse.

Cyclamen *Cyclamen persicum giganteum*

Fall and winter flowering plant develops from an underground corm or tuber. The delicate heart-shaped leaves, mottled paler green, form a full, shapely rosette. Masses of nodding flowers are produced, with one plant bearing up to 30 blooms in one season.

Cyclamen is an excellent flowering plant for cool locations, creating a picture of fragile beauty during the winter months.

Caring For Your Cyclamen

Temperature: Average climate, minimum at night 50-55°F (10-13°C).

Light: Bright indirect light. Prefers humid air.

Watering: Keep soil uniformly moist but not wet.

Fertilizer: Half the recommended strength every two weeks while flowering.

Soil: Add peatmoss to an equal volume of general house plant mix for a humusy and well drained combination.

Uses: Add color during winter months. Single plant for table decoration or close to window; mass several for a larger display.

After flowering: Water and fertilize at the recommended strength every two weeks while new leaves are produced. Gradually reduce watering as leaves die down. Do not fertilize. Allow soil to become dry when all top growth is gone. Remove soil and dead leaves from the dry corm and replant with fresh soil; keep the corm showing above soil to prevent crown rot. Water well. Place in bright indirect light; when new leaves develop, fertilize every 2 weeks. Once flowers appear reduce fertilizer strength to one-half.

From Seed: Sow from August to December. New plants take up to 18 months to flower.

Kenilworth Ivy *Cymbalaria muralis*

Dainty leaves with scalloped edges trail and form a carpet of fresh green. Minute white flowers tinted violet all summer.

Caring For Your Kenilworth Ivy

Temperature: Cool climate, minimum at night 45-55°F (7-13°C).

Light: Partial shade to bright indirect light. Prefers humid air.

Watering: Keep soil moist; not wet.

Fertilize: Every 2-4 weeks while growing vigorously.

Soil: Any general house plant mix or soil that permits good drainage.

Uses: Trailing plant for porch and shaded patio decoration.

After flowering: Water and fertilize while growth is active. Leaves may die back in winter; restart in spring after plant has rested. Resume watering and feeding once new growth starts.

Genista Cytisus canariensis

Golden yellow flowers on spikes adorn the Canary Island Broom. Leaflets in threes create a soft texture on plume-like branches.

Caring For Your Genista

Temperature: Cool climate, minimum at night 45-55°F (7-13°C).

Light: Bright indirect light to full sun. Prefers humid air.

Watering: Soil may become partially dry between waterings.

Fertilize: None needed while your Genista is flowering.

Soil: Any general house plant mix or soil that permits good drainage.

Uses: Seasonal display indoors brings spring in early.

After flowering: Trim off dead flowers and begin to shape the plant. Continue to water; fertilize every 2-4 weeks through the summer months. Move plant outside in spring. Continue trimming Genista at intervals as needed through September. Keep it out of doors until temperatures fall to 40°F (5°C). Move to a protected place with bright indirect light, maintaining only 40°F (5°C) until January. Then increase temperature to 45° (7°) to encourage flowering. Move Genista back indoors when flower buds are well developed. If low winter temperature cannot be held, flowering will be more spread and irregular.

Rose Heath

Erica gracilis

Thousands of miniature rose pink bells cover this dense, shrubby plant in fall and winter, partially concealing the attractive needle-like foliage.

Caring For Your Rose Heath

Temperature: Average climate, minimum at night 50-55°F (10-13°C).

Light: Bright indirect light to full sun. Prefers humid air.

Watering: Soil may become partially dry between waterings.

Fertilizer: None needed while Rose Heath is flowering.

Soil: An acid mix of peatmoss with half as much or an equal volume of general house plant mix.

Uses: Late season decoration on porch or patio. Adds color indoors as winter approaches.

After flowering: Trim shoots to about half their length. Plunge in the ground in spring, water regularly and fertilize every month through summer. Continue to trim new growth as desired until early September. Flowers develop late in summer.

Persian Violet *Exacum affine*

Low growing plant about 6 inches high, liberally sprinkled with eyecatching bluish-lavender blossoms which keep on coming through summer and fall. Stems and leaves are crisp, bright green.

Caring For Your Persian Violet

Temperature: Average to warm climate, minimum at night 60-65°F (16-18°C).

Light: Partial shade to bright indirect light. Prefers humid air.

Watering: Keep soil uniformly moist but not wet.

Fertilize: Every 2 weeks.

Soil: Add peatmoss to an equal volume of general house plant mix for a humusy and well drained combination.

Uses: Attractive small decorator item for table, shelf, windowsill—anywhere with sufficient light to maintain leaf color.

After flowering: Persian Violet will continue to grow in a greenhouse; otherwise, plant will die back in winter and should be discarded.

Blue Daisy *Felicia amelloides*

Sprightly color and daisy freshness make *Felicia* an appealing choice for a winter windowsill plant. Equally suited to outdoor culture on a balcony or patio.

Caring For Your Blue Daisy

Temperature: Average climate, minimum at night 50-55°F (10-13°C).

Light: Bright indirect light to full sun.

Watering: Keep soil uniformly moist but not wet.

Fertilize: Every 2-4 weeks.

Soil: Any general house plant mix or soil that permits good drainage.

Uses: Decorator value for any room with sufficient light. Use on low table, floor or window box. Flowers almost constantly when dead blossoms are pruned.

Lady's Eardrops *Fuchsia x hybrida "Springtime"*

Pendulous blooms in rosy red and white hang gracefully from trailing branches. The attractive leaves are borne in pairs.

Caring For Your Fuchsia

Temperature: Cool climate, minimum at night 50-55°F (10-13°C), days not exceeding 70° (21°).

Light: Partial shade to bright diffused light. Prefers humid air.

Watering: Keep soil uniformly moist but not wet.

Fertilizer: Every 2-4 weeks while growing and flowering.

Soil: Any general house plant mix or soil that permits good drainage.

Uses: Porch, patio and shaded outdoor areas in summer. Good for hanging baskets, windowboxes, planters. Use as bedding plant where summers are relatively cool (e.g. Pacific Northwest).

After flowering: Gradually reduce watering frequency and allow soil to dry out more between waterings as leaves die and while Fuchsia rests during winter. Reduce feeding to once every 4-8 weeks while resting, or adjust frequency to match growth rate (slower during darker winter months).

New growth begins in spring. Prune as desired. Gradually resume more frequent watering and feeding.

Lipstick Vine *Aeschynanthus lobbianus*

Superb flowering plant with large, glossy leaves and tubular shaped red blooms. Trailing stems hang 1-3 feet long.

Caring For Your Lipstick Vine

Temperature: Average warm climate, minimum at night 62-65°F (17-18°C).

Light: Plenty of light though shade from full sun in summer and outdoors. Prefers humid air.

Watering: Keep soil uniformly moist but not wet.

Fertilize: Every month while making vigorous new growth after flowering. Every other month in fall and winter.

Soil: Any good house plant mix, or add peatmoss for a more humusy combination.

Uses: Smaller plants for table decoration. Hanging baskets.

After flowering: Prune back shoots to 6 inches for strong new growth. Requires high light for flower development. Flowers in spring after cooler and drier resting period during winter.

Goldfish Plant *Columnea lepidocaula*

This species will flower almost continually with sufficient light and normal indoor conditions. Blooms are an attractive orange, shaded to yellow, and with soft fuzzy texture.

Caring For Your Goldfish Plant

Temperature: Average to warm climate, minimum at night 62-65°F (17-18°C).

Light: Plenty of light though shade from full sun in summer and outdoors.

Watering: Keep soil uniformly moist but not wet.

Fertilize: Every month.

Soil: Any good house plant mix, or add peatmoss for a more humusy combination.

Uses: Table decoration and hanging baskets.

After flowering: Keep shoots growing vigorously in high light situation. Do not Pinch or prune. Flowers in spring and summer after cooler and drier resting period during winter.

45

HYPOCYRTA "TROPICANA"

Outstanding variety of Pouch Flower, having larger leaves, and flowers pale yellow striped and spotted a deep maroon.

Caring For Your Hypocyrta

Temperature: Average to warm climate, minimum at night 62-65°F (17-18°C).

Light: Plenty of light though shade from full sun in summer and outdoors. Prefers humid air.

Watering: Keep soil uniformly moist but not wet.

Fertilize: Every month while making vigorous new growth; every other month in fall and winter.

Soil: Any good house plant mix, or add peatmoss for a more humusy combination.

Uses: On table, shelf or windowsill. Larger plants with pendulous stems good in hanging baskets.

After flowering: Prune back shoots to 6 inches to encourage strong new growth. Leaves may be lost as plant enters a winter dormancy period; reduce watering frequency and withhold fertilizer until growth restarts in spring. Requires high light for flower initiation and development. If growth has continued through winter, Hypocyrta will start flowering in spring; after dormancy, flowers develop in summer on new growth.

MINIATURE POUCH FLOWER
Hypocyrta wettsteinii

Ideal hanging basket plant with diminutive waxy leaves in pairs and vibrant orange blooms terminating in a bright yellow lip.

LACE FLOWER VINE
Episcia dianthiflora
Low growing relative of the African Violet with fringed white flowers nestled among the wooly leaves. Creeping runners are easily rooted.

Flame Violets

Caring For Your Episcia

Temperature: Average to warm climate, minimum at night 60-65°F (16-18°C).

Light: Bright indirect light; prefers humid air.

Watering: Keep soil uniformly moist but not wet; avoid splashing water onto foliage. Use tepid water.

Fertilize: Every 4-6 weeks.

Soil: Add peatmoss to an equal volume of general house plant mix for a humusy and well drained combination.

Uses: Small specimen plants for shelf, windowsill, hanging basket. Ground cover. Dish gardens, terrariums.

After flowering: Leaves may be lost if temperatures fall below 60°F (16°C), and in low humidity conditions prevalent indoors during winter. Dormancy is induced with 50°F (10°C) temperatures. Episcias grow back once they warm up again. They require plenty of light for flower initiation and development.

PINK BROCADE
Episcia 'Pink Brocade'
Best loved of the many colorful Episcia varieties. Leaves glisten with pink and pale olive-green iridescence; the scarlet flowers make a striking contrast.

47

African Violets

Saintpaulia ionantha

Traditional flowering houseplant; blooms continually with sufficient light.

Caring For Your African Violets

Temperature: Average to warm climate, minimum at night 60-65°F (16-18°C).

Light: Indirect sunlight or partial shade. Prefers humid air.

Watering: Keep soil moist but not wet; avoid splashing water onto foliage.

Fertilize: Apply at half the recommended strength every month.

Soil: Add peatmoss to an equal volume of general house plant mix for a humusy and well drained soil.

Uses: Specimen for table or shelf, fine in kitchen or bathroom where air is humid.

After flowering: Use regular watering and fertilization. Requires plenty of light for flower development; **too much** light can result in yellow foliage.

Dauphin Violet

◀ *Streptocarpus saxorum*

Pale lilac flowers bloom above the velvety green foliage of this exquisitely delicate creeping plant.

Caring For Your Dauphin Violet

Temperature: Average climate, minimum at night 60-65°F (16-18°C): cooler during winter months (55-60°F, 13-16°C).

Light: Indirect sunlight or partial shade, full sun in winter.

Watering: Keep soil moist but not wet; avoid splashing foliage. During the winter soil may be allowed to dry between waterings.

Fertilize: Apply at half the recommended strength every month while growing.

Soil: Any good house plant mix, or add peatmoss for a more humusy and well drained combination.

Uses: Decorative small plant for table, shelf, windowsill or hanging container.

After flowering: Maintain active growth with regular watering and feeding. Requires plenty of light for flowering. Growth resumes after a brief cooler resting period in winter.

MINIATURE SLIPPER PLANT
Sinningia concinna

Sinningia pusilla

The Miniature Sinningias

Charming little plants with tube-shaped flowers in pastel colors; rarely exceed 2 inches high (5 cm). The perfect choice for a flowering terrarium plant.

Caring For Your Miniature Sinningia

Temperature: Average to warm climate, minimum at night 60-65°F (16-18°C).

Light: Bright indirect light or partial shade. Prefers humid air.

Watering: Keep soil uniformly moist but not wet.

Sinningia species

Fertilize: Every 1-2 months.

Soil: Add peatmoss to an equal volume of general house plant mix for a humusy and well drained combination.

Uses: Tiny decorator item for terrarium, brandy snifter, or other enclosed transparent planter.

After flowering: Maintain active growth with regular watering and feeding. Miniature Sinningias require plenty of light for flower initiation and development. Plants may become dormant in winter: reduce frequency of water and fertilizer applications until new growth starts after midwinter.

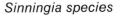

49

◄ **GLOXINIA**
Sinningia speciosa
Deep royal purple flowers grace this Gloxinia variety. Double and bicolor types are also available.

Lush, velvety crimson flowers are held above soft oval leaves, to make a truly elegant flowering plant. Each blossom lasts 2-4 days, and a succession of flowers gives lasting color. **(Below)**
▼

Gloxinias

Caring For Your Gloxinia

Temperature: Average to warm climate, minimum at night 60-65°F (16-18°C).

Light: Indirect sunlight and partial shade.

Watering: Keep soil uniformly moist but not wet; avoid splashing water onto foliage.

Fertilize: Every 1-2 months.

Soil: Add peatmoss to an equal volume of general house plant mix for a humusy and well drained combination.

Uses: Specimen for table or shelf, adds color to any room.

After flowering: Reduce watering frequency when leaves start to die down; stop applying fertilizer at this time. Gloxinia tubers rest for 2-4 months, with completely dry soil. As soon as new growth appears, repot in fresh soil and resume watering and fertilization. Tubers flower in about 3 months;

50

Tahitian Bridal Veil Gibasis geniculata

Slender trailing stems bear many deep green leaves and innumerable tiny white flowers which close in the evening. An excellent full hanging basket plant for patio or sunny window.

Caring For Your Tahitian Bridal Veil

Temperature: Warm climate, minimum at night 60-65°F (16-18°C).

Light: Bright diffused light or partial shade.

Watering: Soil may dry out between waterings.

Fertilize: Apply at half the recommended strength every 1-2 months.

Soil: Any general house plant mix or soil that permits good drainage.

Uses: Hanging basket and trailing plant for windowsill or shelf. Flowers almost continuously once established and with adequate light.

Wax Plants

Thick succulent leaves on trailing or twining stems provide a fine background for the clusters of fragrant blossoms.

Caring For Your Wax Plant

Temperature: Average to warm climate, minimum at night 60-65°F (16-18°C). Tolerates as cool as 45°F (7°C) for short periods.

Light: Bright indirect light or partial shade; avoid full midday sun.

Watering: Soil may dry out between waterings.

Fertilize: Every 2-3 months.

Soil: Any general house plant mix or soil that permits good drainage.

Uses: Small specimens for table, shelf, windowsill. Larger plants in hanging baskets, or to climb on wires, bark or pole.

After flowering: Do not remove flowering spur (old flower stem) since new flowers will form here next year. Keep cooler in winter (55-60°F, 13-16°C); reduce watering frequency to match slower growth rate. Wax Plant needs very bright indirect light for flower initiation.

KRIMSON PRINCESS® ▲
Hoya carnosa rubra (Pat. 3105)

WAX PLANT
Hoya minata ▼

Snowball Plant Hydrangea macrophylla

Large flowers in globe-shaped clusters top the woody stems and quilted foliage. Blue flowers develop in acid soil (about pH 5.0), pink blossoms in more neutral conditions (pH 6.5).

Caring For Your Hydrangea

Temperature: Average climate, minimum at night 50-55°F (10-13°C).

Light: Bright indirect light; avoid full sun while in flower.

Watering: Keep soil uniformly moist but not wet.

Fertilize: None needed while Hydrangea is flowering.

Soil: Any general house plant mix or soil that permits good drainage.

Uses: Attractive specimen to add color to any room or patio. Flowers last 1-2 months.

After flowering: Water regularly and fertilize every 1-2 months through summer. Flower buds form at 60-65°F (16-18°C). They continue development through winter dormancy at 40-45°F (5-7°C) in darkness for at least 6 weeks, or through winter outdoors where Hydrangeas are hardy.

53

Impatiens

IMPATIENS
Impatiens walleriana sultani

Peppermint striped flowers grace this attractive plant. The flowers contrast well with deeply veined green leaves.

Caring For Your Impatiens

Temperature: Average to cool climate, minimum at night 50-60°F (10-16°C).

Light: Bright indirect light or full sun. Partial shade out of doors.

Watering: Keep soil uniformly moist but not wet.

Fertilize: Every 2-4 weeks while growing vigorously.

Soil: Add peatmoss to an equal volume of general house plant mix for a humusy and well drained combination.

Uses: Specimen plants, great for windowsills, porch and patio decoration. Hanging baskets, containers, mixed plant groups. Outdoor bedding plant for shaded area. Flowers continuously with adequate light.

IMPATIENS
Impatiens walleriana sultani

A mixture of Impatiens in one basket created this splash of color. Try different color combinations for more interesting effects.

IMPATIENS
Impatiens hawkeri hybrid

Hybrids of *I. hawkeri* all have interesting zoned and variegated foliage, with colorful leaf centers of yellow, pink, or white.

Caring For Your Impatiens See page 54

Blue Angel Tears Ilysanthes grandiflora

This relatively new plant is quickly becoming popular for brightly lighted spots. The tiny violet-blue and white flowers are produced continuously among the bright green, dime-sized leaves on long, trailing stems.

Caring For Your Blue Angel Tears

Temperature: Average climate, minimum at night 50-55°F (10-13°C).

Light: Full sun or bright indirect light. Prefers humid air.

Watering: Never allow soil to dry out.

Fertilize: Every 2 weeks; less often when growth slows.

Soil: Any general house plant mix or soil that permits good drainage.

Uses: Hanging basket or trailing plant for high light areas. Good in humid climates. Flowers continuously with adequate light and constant moisture.

Kalanchoe

◀ **DWARF PURPLE KALANCHOE**
Kalanchoe pumila
Compact plant with leaves lightly shaded silvery white. Four-petaled flowers are borne in clusters and range in color from red through pale pink and violet.

Caring For Your Kalanchoe

Temperature: Average climate, minimum at night 50-60°F (10-16°C). Tolerates as low as 40°F (5°C) for short periods.

Light: Bright indirect light or full sun.

Watering: Soil may dry out between waterings.

Fertilizer: None needed while Kalanchoe is in flower. Fertilize every 2-4 weeks after flowering and when growing rapidly.

Soil: Any general house plant mix or soil that permits good drainage.

Uses: Small or medium sized specimen plant during the prolonged flowering period. Attractive foliage at all times, making a handsome patio or porch plant in summer after all danger of frost is past.

Kalanchoe ▶
'Fuerball'

◀ Kalanchoe 'Melodie'
New hybrid variety kalanchoe. Compact growing with large, glossy scalloped leaves and masses of peach colored flowers. The pointed flower buds open continuously for several weeks, providing a long-lasting floral display.

After flowering: Trim off faded blossoms and continue to water regularly when soil dries. Fertilize every 2-4 weeks as new growth begins. Trim plant to encourage compact growth and a bushy form. Cuttings for new plants may be taken during the summer when growth is rapid and long days prevent the formation of flower buds. To flower again, Kalanchoe must have at least 14 hours of continuous total darkness nightly. Flowers will open about 3-4 months after a long night schedule is begun.

◀ Kalanchoe blossfeldiana 'Tom Thumb'

57

King Jasmine _Jasminum rex_

Dazzling white star-shaped blossoms adorn this bushy, vining plant. Glossy, dark green leaves make it attractive when not in flower. This jasmine flowers for 4-8 weeks in winter.

Caring For Your King Jasmine

Temperature: Average to warm climate, minimum at night 60-65°F (16-18°C).

Light: Full sun or bright indirect light. Best in cooler climates. Prefers humid air.

Watering: Keep soil uniformly moist but not wet.

Fertilize: Every 1-2 months while growing vigorously.

Soil: Any general house plant mix or soil that permits good drainage.

Uses: Specimen plant, beautiful when in full bloom; even though individual flowers drop quickly, the rapid succession assures continued display. Makes a good patio plant in summer.

After flowering: Continue to water and fertilize regularly through spring and summer. As growth slows in fall, reduce watering frequency and apply less fertilizer. Trim plant in spring before new growth starts; provide support for vining stems. Requires plenty of light for successful reflowering.

Lantana L. camara

Summer flowers are pastel orange, yellow and pink shades. Foliage exudes a strong, pleasant odor when crushed.

Caring For Your Lantana

Temperature: Average climate, minimum at night 50-55°F (7-13°C).

Light: Full sun or bright indirect light.

Watering: Soil may dry out between waterings.

Fertilize: Every month while growing.

Soil: Any general house plant mix or soil that permits good drainage.

Uses: Small specimen shrub for indoor or outdoor use. Becomes woody and grows to about 3 feet tall.

After flowering: Reduce watering and fertilizing frequency as growth slows in fall and winter. Keep in full sun. Trim to shape in spring. Resume regular water and fertilizer applications to match increased growth rate.

Egyptian Star Cluster Pentas lanceolata

Rose colored flower heads contrast with the soft green foliage of this tropical African plant. Also available in white and salmon shades. Shrubby plant flowers in fall and winter.

Caring For Your Pentas

Temperature: Average to warm climate, minimum at night 60-65°F (16-18°C).

Light: Bright indirect light, full sun in winter.

Watering: Keep soil moist but not wet.

Fertilize: Every month while growing

Soil: Any general house plant mix or soil that permits good drainage.

Uses: Flowering plant for indoors and out. Fine as filler plant between tall specimens in interior landscapes with adequate light.

After flowering: Continue to water and fertilize regularly through spring and summer. Trim and prune in spring; take cuttings at this time, too. Requires plenty of light for successful reflowering.

59

Orchids

◄ QUEEN OF ORCHIDS
Cattleya hybrid

Dramatic, regal flowers open in summer and fall, last for several weeks. Fine specimen plant for high humidity area and close to window where nights are cooler. *Cattleya* grows from swollen pseudobulbs.

Caring For Your Orchids

Soil: Add at least an equal volume of chopped fern fiber or sphagnum to general house plant mix for a coarse, humusy combination with ability to retain water and nutrients.

Fertilize: Every month with a high nitrogen mixture (e.g. 2:1:1 ratio).

CATTLEYA

Temperature: Average, night minimum 55-60°F (13-16°C).

Light: Full sun or bright indirect light; avoid burning sunlight. Humid air a must.

Watering: Water thoroughly as soon as soil is dry.

After flowering: Reduce watering and fertilizing frequency as *Cattleya* rests. When new growth starts, resume regular applications. Flowers develop with adequate light and humidity.

PAPHIOPEDILUM

Temperature: Average to cool, night minimum 45-55°F (7-13°C).

Light: Partial or shade. Humid air a must.

Watering: Keep soil uniformly moist but not wet.

After flowering: Continue to keep soil uniformly moist; do not saturate it. Too much light inhibits flowering and causes yellowed foliage in *Paphiopedilum*.

Cattleya hybrid ▲

◀ LADY-SLIPPER ORCHID
Paphiopedilum x nerissa

The striking, waxy-looking flowers last as long as 3-4 months in optimum conditions. Commonly called CYPRIPEDIUM, this orchid is shade loving; it grows in moist, humid conditions.

Cattleya hybrid ▼

◄ SHOW GERANIUM
Pelargonium x domesticum

Distinctive geranium variety preferring cool daytime temperatures (65°F, 18°C); keep soil evenly moist at all times. The large flowers may be striped and spotted, are often reminiscent of clusters of azalea blooms.

SCENTED GERANIUM
Pelargonium graveolens **(Below left)**

Although its flowers are not spectacular, the leaves of scented geraniums yield alluring odors when crushed. Among the scented geraniums are those with foliage fragrant like roses, lemon, mint, pine, and several spices.

Geraniums

Caring For Your Geraniums

Temperature: Average to cool climate, minimum at night 40-50°F (5-10°C).

Light: Bright diffused light, full sun where possible.

Watering: Soil may dry out between waterings.

Fertilize: Every month while growing vigorously.

Soil: Any general house plant mix or soil that permits good drainage.

Uses: Windowsill plants, or for containers on porch and patio. Hanging baskets (Ivy Geraniums). Outdoor bedding plants (Zonals).

After flowering: Geraniums will continue to grow in brightly lighted conditions. Cuttings can be taken from new growth and maintained indoors through winter. Leaves may die back in fall unless light is sufficient for continued growth. As leaves drop, reduce watering frequency and stop fertilizing. Store geranium roots dry, either in the pots or shake off the soil

ZONAL GERANIUMS
Pelargonium x hortorum
The most frequently grown of all geranium types, valued for their flower quality and abundance, and tolerant of adverse conditions. Many varieties have leaves marked with a distinct band or zone in a darker color.

IVY GERANIUM
Pelargonium peltatum
Crisp, shiny leaves on trailing stems characterize the ivy geranium. This type prefers humid air. Cut off dead flowers for continuous blooming throughout summer.

and keep in a dry, frost-free, dark place. Restart stored geraniums in late winter when new growth first appears: gradually increase water applications and resume fertilizing when first leaves are fully expanded.

63

◀ **ALUMINUM PLANT**
Pilea cadierei

MOON VALLEY
Pilea 'Moon Valley'
(Below)
▼

Pilea

More familiar as foliage plants, the Pileas will flower when given enough light. Pink or yellow blossoms enhance their decorative value.

Caring For Your Pilea

Temperature: Average to warm climate, minimum at night 60-65°F (16-18°C).

Light: Partial shade or bright indirect light.

Watering: Keep soil uniformly moist but not wet.

Fertilize: Every 2 months.

Soil: Any general house plant mix or soil that permits good drainage.

Uses: Small specimen plant for table, shelf or windowsill. Dish garden, terrarium plant. Spreading varieties for hanging baskets.

After flowering: Trim off the faded blossoms and prune plants to shape as desired and to encourage branching. With adequate light, Pilea flowers in summer and fall.

64

Velvet Swedish Ivy *Plectranthus oertendahlii*

Caring For Your Velvet Swedish Ivy

Temperature: Average to warm climate, minimum at night 60-65°F (16-18°C). Tolerates as low as 40°F (5°C) for short periods.

Light: Partial shade or bright diffused light.

Watering: Keep soil evenly moist but not wet.

Fertilize: Every one to two months.

Soil: Any general house plant mix or soil that permits good drainage.

Uses: Full, spreading specimen plant for hanging baskets. Smaller plants add interest to low table or windowsill.

▲ A relative of the coleus, this lovely plant is valued for its lush, silver-veined foliage as well as pale, lavender pink flowers. Pinch stem tips to encourage fullness.

Polygonum *Polygonum capitatum*

Caring For Your Polygonum

Temperature: Average to warm climate; minimum at night 50-55°F (10-13°C). Tolerates as low as 40°F (5°C) for prolonged periods.

Light: Bright indirect light or full sun.

Watering: Keep soil evenly moist but not wet.

Fertilize: Every 2-4 weeks while growing vigorously.

Soil: Any general house plant mix or soil that permits good drainage.

Uses: Dependable flowering plant outdoors in summer, or indoors with sufficient light. Plant may become dormant in winter under low light, dropping leaves and ceasing active growth. When dormant cut back to 6 inches (15 cm) and reduce watering. Resume regular watering and fertilization in spring.

Creeping stems bring forth globe-shaped, pale pink flowers to ¾ inches (2 cm) across. A profuse bloomer in summer and occasionally at other times if light is adequate.

Strawberry Begonia _Saxifraga sarmentosa_

Summer blooming houseplant producing new plantlets on runners which provide additional interest.

Temperature: Average to cool climate; minimum at night 40-50°F (5-10°C).

Light: Bright indirect light or full sun indoors. Partial shade outdoors.

Watering: Soil may dry out between waterings.

Fertilize: Every 3-4 months.

Soil: Any general houseplant mix or soil that permits good drainage.

Uses: Small specimen or hanging basket plant flowering naturally in spring or summer with adequate light. Patio plant for sheltered location.

German Ivy

Senecio mikanioides

Fragrant, yellow flowers in spring and summer contrast with the fresh green leaves of this old-fashioned plant.

Caring For Your German Ivy

Temperature: Average climate; minimum at night 50-60°F (10-16°C).

Light: Bright indirect sunlight or partial shade.

Watering: Keep soil evenly moist but not wet.

Fertilize: Every 1-2 months at half the recommended rate.

Soil: Any general house plant mix or soil that permits good drainage.

Uses: Climbing or trailing accent plant. Suitable for hanging baskets and will grow well in plain water.

Oxalis

◄ WINDOW BOX OXALIS
Oxalis rubra alba

Bulb forming houseplant used primarily outdoors in warmer regions. Triangular leaflets lend interest when flowers are not present.

Caring For Your Oxalis

Temperature: Average to cool climate; minimum at night 50-60°F (10-16°C).

Light: Bright indirect light or full sun. Partial shade outdoors.

Watering: Soil may dry out between waterings.

Fertilize: Monthly while growing rapidly.

Soil: Any general house plant mix or soil that permits good drainage.

Uses: Color accent for windowsill or other well lit area. Large specimens as hanging baskets or in window boxes.

After flowering: Oxalis generally flower in winter and spring, although they may be used as summer annuals. The bulbs benefit from a rest period of several months immediately after flowering. Remove blooms as they fade and gradually decrease watering frequency. Do not fertilize. During this dormant period the soil should be kept fairly dry and the temperature preferably cool (50-60°F, 10-16°C) as leaves die down. Repotting and division of large plants should be done during this time. New growth may begin within several months or can be initiated by resuming regular watering and fertilization.

◄ BRAZIL OXALIS
Oxalis braziliensis

Poinsettia *Euphorbia pulcherrima*

Traditional holiday favorites since their introduction from Mexico over 150 years ago. Newly developed hybrids hold their flower bracts for several months.

Caring For Your Poinsettia

Temperature: Average to warm climate, minimum at night 55-65°F (13-18°C).

Light: Bright indirect light or full sun.

Watering: Soil may dry out between waterings.

Fertilize: Every month. Inadequate fertilization can cause leaves to drop.

Soil: Any general house plant mix or soil that permits good drainage.

Uses: Decorative holiday plant for display on tables or as a large floor specimen. Can be used in hanging baskets with spectacular effect.

After flowering: Continue to water and fertilize regularly. Provide maximum light to prevent lower leaves from yellowing and dropping. In early spring, repot into a larger container and trim to encourage strong new growth which will develop a full plant. For best growth and subsequent blooming, poinsettias should be grown outdoors in full sun during summer. In fall, move the plants back indoors.

Poinsettias flower naturally in response to the longer nights of fall. They must have more than 12 hours of uninterrupted complete darkness nightly, from approximately October 1 until December 1, to flower for the holidays. After the bracts have begun to develop, the plant may be returned to normal indoor conditions.

As poinsettias are highly light sensitive, precautions should be taken to assure that the dark cycle is never broken. The glare of a street light or light entering beneath a door is often sufficient to prevent buds from forming.

69

FAIRY PRIMOSE
Primula malacoides

Small perennial plants with long-lasting flowers frequently having 'eyes' in a contrasting color.

Caring For Your Primrose

Temperature: Average to cool, minimum at night 50-60°F (10-16°C). Tolerates as low as 45-55°F (7-13°C) for prolonged periods.

Light: Partial shade or bright indirect light. Prefers humid air.

Watering: Soil should remain evenly moist but not wet.

Fertilize: Monthly from after blooming until dormancy.

Soil: Add peat moss to an equal volume of general houseplant mix for a humusy and well drained combination.

After flowering: Primula x polyantha is quite hardy and may be reflowered; Primula malacoides is best raised as an annual and discarded after flowering. For Polyanthus Primroses, continue to water and fertilize regularly

throughout the growing season. They may be kept outdoors in a sheltered location during summer and moved indoors before the frost. During the winter, maintain the plants in an unheated room, or on a cool windowsill or enclosed porch, keeping the soil moist. Primulas flower any time from autumn to spring.

Primroses

POLYANTHUS PRIMOSE *Primula x polyantha*

POLYANTHA ROSE *Rosa x polyantha*

Compact growing rose to 15 inches (38 cm) tall with clusters of 1-2 inch (3-5 cm) diameter blossoms. A handsome plant for Mother's Day.

Roses

aring For Your Rose

mperature: Average climate; minimum night 50-55°F (10-13°C).

ght: Bright indirect light to full sun.

atering: Keep soil evenly moist but ot wet.

ertilize: Monthly while growing rapidly spring and summer.

oil: Any general house plant mix or soil at permits good drainage.

ses: Indoor specimen plant for sunny ndowsill or other well lit area. ecorative patio or balcony pot plant spring and summer.

fter flowering: Continue to water and rtilize regularly while growing actively. rowth is best when potted roses are aced outdoors in full sun during the immer. Many roses benefit from a ol "rest" period during winter; prune nd repot at this time. Miniature roses are

MINIATURE ROSE
Rosa chinensis hybrida

Tiny roses to 12 inches (30 cm) high bearing single blooms ½ to 1 inch (1-3 cm) across and equally miniature leaves.

ery cold hardy and may be rested in pots left outdoors throughout the winter. They may so be kept actively growing on a sunny windowsill. Polyantha roses are less hardy and ould not be left outdoors over winter except in milder climates where temperatures do ot drop below 20°F (-6°C). These roses are best overwintered in a bright unheated room enclosed porch where growth will nearly stop while the plant rests.

Sedum

CHRISTMAS CHEERS *Sedum rubrotinctum*

Summer blooming succulent with leaf tips turning deep red in full sun. Grows rapidly and may be rooted from single leaves placed in damp sand.

Caring For Your Sedum

Temperature: Average to cool climate; minimum at night 50-60°F (10-16°C). Tolerates lower or higher temperatures ranging from 40-100°F (5-38°C).

Light: Bright indirect light to full sun. Leaves become widely spaced without sufficient light.

Fertilize: Monthly in spring and summer, every 3-4 months in fall and winter.

Soil: Any general house plant mix or soil that permits good drainage.

Uses: Hanging basket plant in bright window or on patio or balcony in summer. Small plants in dish gardens with cacti and other succulents.

The Flowering Response

One or more environmental factors frequently triggers the flowering response of all plants. A prime example is that of *daylength,* or *photoperiod,* yet many other indoor plants like the gesneriads respond to *light intensity* rather than to the actual length of day or night. *Temperature* is a modifying factor which can affect both the flower initiation response and the later development of the bud before and after it emerges from its protective sheath. The plant's *maturity* and *nutritional level* can also affect its flowering response.

1. Photoperiod

While the name refers to the length of day, it is in fact the hours of continuous darkness, or night, which effects flower initiation in some plants. Best known examples of short day plants (i.e. long nights) are those which flower naturally from fall to winter (chrysanthemum and poinsettia) when days are shorter. *Short day plants* need from 11 to 15 hours of uninterrupted darkness, nightly for generally 6-10 weeks (depending on variety) before they will be completely conditioned to flower. It is advisable to continue darkness treatments nightly until the buds begin to show color before the plant may be safely returned to normal light conditions. Stopping nightly darkness treatments too soon may result in sparse or delayed flowering or even no flowering at all. Enclosing your short day plant in a light proof closet nightly is one way to provide the darkness treatment necessary for flowering. *Long day plants,* on the other hand, need shorter nights and longer days; they also may be brought into flower by breaking the dark period artificially such as by leaving the plant in a room which is kept lit during the evening hours. Spring flowered beauties like calceolarias, as well as the majority of annual bedding plants, are examples of long day plants. *Day neutral* or *indeterminate* (daylength) response plants do not show any definite reaction by flowering in either long or short day conditions. Many indoor flowering plants fall into this category.

2. Light Intensity

Some plants will form flowers when the light is sufficiently bright, regardless of whether they are getting 11 or 15 hours of it. You can enjoy year round blossoms on these plants—for example, the African violet.

3. Temperature

This acts as a major modifier of plant responses; for instance, a definite short-day or long-day flowering response will take place only within a certain range of temperatures. This explains why poinsettias often refuse to flower in the heat of midsummer even with the appropriate length of darkness. Chrysanthemum flowering is also delayed at temperatures above 80°F (26°C). A number of indoor flowering plants need different temperatures for the different stages of initiation and development of flowers. These include the bulb and corm plants (hyacinth, daffodil, crocus, tulip, Easter lily), Christmas cactus, azalea and hydrangea. For example, azalea buds form during the heat of summer and early fall; low temperatures are required for the new buds to develop uniformly; and, once they are developed to a certain point, an increase in temperature effects their opening.

4. Maturity

Some plants will flower regardless of daylength or temperature, provided these are within the normal range. Their flowering response depends largely upon the age or maturity of the plants. Examples here are cineraria, geranium, Christmas cherry and ornamental pepper; the specific size or age of plant varies with the individual variety and environment.

5. Moisture and Nutrition

Plant responses to the various environmental factors can be modified by abnormal growth which can result from poor or unbalanced nutrition, or from excessive over- or under-watering. For example, an overdose of nitrogen (from a nitrogen rich fertilizer) can stimulate excessive soft leafy growth which will delay flowering. When other factors are conducive to flower bud formation, over-watering can prevent some or all buds from developing and opening normally. Examples of plants susceptible to this are: the wax plant *(Hoya)*, azalea, or Christmas cactus. These plants need a period of hardening (strengthening) in summer, with reduced watering frequency, for successful budding. A pot-bound plant often responds by producing flower buds, because it is naturally hardened by scarce water and nutrients in its pot-bound condition.

Pests and Diseases of Indoor Plants

The most common indoor *pests* are spider mites, scale insects, whitefly and aphids; thrips and leaf miner show up on some indoor flowering plants. Soil pests, like springtails and fungus gnats occur on all container-grown plants where the soil or container has not been properly sterilized.

Many of the insecticides recommended below will severely damage the tender blossoms on flowering plants; it is best to try to avoid chemical sprays on plants while they are flowering. The safest compound, one which is derived from natural sources, is Pyrethrum—reasonably effective against many common insect pests and also relatively harmless to flowers. The other compounds are safe when used with care on green plants, or on flowering plants before the flowers open.

Despite the best control programs employed by growers and retailers, it sometimes happens that a new plant harbors pests whose eggs have survived to hatch in your home conditions. A period of isolation (10-14 days) may be the answer. Yet some pests may not show up for a longer time, being present in minute numbers until the indoor climate becomes more favorable; for example, spider mites thrive in dry air, so they may not become evident until the humid season is past.

Regular and frequent checking for abnormal growth and insects can be combined with your checks for watering needs. Most pests lurk under leaves and close to the growing tip where tissue is softest, and most of them can be washed off with a spray of water. Several washes over a period of two or three weeks, plus isolation for the infested plant to prevent the pest moving to others, generally eliminates the problem. Chemical sprays are not pleasant to use, and are recommended only for outdoor application, if possible. Those sold in aerosol form are hazardous, not only to the general environment, but to the plant tissue which will be burned by the propellant if the nozzle is held too close: a distance of 24 inches should be safe. Ferns are super-sensitive to all forms of chemical spray, and infested fronds are best removed and destroyed.

Diseases on indoor plants show up when plants are kept in a humid environment, or when dead and dying tissues remain on the plant to harbor fungal and bacterial growth. The diseases most likely to be encountered are Botrytis, the gray mold fungus that invades dead and dying tissues, and soft leaf spot or crown rot fungi which thrive in moist atmospheres. The best cure is to remove affected parts, and avoid splashing the plant when you water; give more space for air circulation, or move infected plants to a drier place.

Pest	Typical damage	Control
SPIDER MITES	Tiny white or yellow spots on leaves, later becoming mottled and dusty. Fine webs under leaves and in growing tips. Leaves may curl up. Thrive in dry climates.	Wash and spray plant with clean warm water, several times in 2-3 weeks. Spray Kelthane or other miticide, every 5-7 days, three times for complete control.*
SCALE INSECTS	Clusters of green to brown scales under leaves and on stems, plus mottling of foliage when seen against the light.	Rub off the scales, or wipe over with cotton soaked in rubbing alcohol (check plant for tolerance by treating one leaf, then wait 24 hours)—this kills adult insects. Spray Malathion.*
MEALY BUGS	Cottony white secretions along stems and under leaves. Flat insects move, though slowly.	Wash off insects and secretions with clean warm water. Kill by wiping off with rubbing alcohol—first check plant's tolerance. Spray with insecticide containing Pyrethrum, Malathion or Diazinon.*
WHITE FLIES	Tiny white moths fly up when plant is disturbed; larvae suck plant juices, causing general weakening. Thrive in dry climates, generally on flowering plants and annuals.	Wash off the tiny wingless larvae. Adult whitefly controlled with spray of insecticide containing Pyrethrum or Malathion.*
APHIDS	Green, red or black insects visibly sucking plant juices, cause small, distorted, weak growth.	Wash whole plant several times. Spray with insecticide containing Pyrethrum or Malathion.*
LEAF MINER	Irregular yellow, cream or brown channels across leaves; weakened growth.	Spray with insecticide containing Malathion.*
THRIPS	Thin, papery scars on leaves remain after these insects have sucked plant juices.	Control Thrips with insecticide containing Pyrethrum, Malathion.*
SPRING-TAILS	Transparent jumping insects at soil surface. Some damage to lower plant tissues.	Drench soil (water it on) with mild vinegar solution to discourage springtails (1-2 tsp per pint). Or apply solution of Pyrethrum Malathion to soil.*
FUNGUS GNATS	Tiny black insects fly up in clouds when disturbed. White maggots (larvae) come to soil surface when it is watered. Feed on dead material in soil, then live roots.	Drench soil (water it on) with solution containing Pyrethrum or Malathion.*

*Check with your supplier for compounds recommended as safe. Use only those registered in your state for the control of these pests.

Disorders of Indoor Plants

The reasons for plant disorders often seem conflicting; for example, a wilting plant can be caused by too much water or too little. If something is amiss with your plant, first check the soil; this is your guide to the most frequent troubles. Less often are the problems caused by too much or too little light: and other plant troubles are brought on by very dry air (usually in winter), hot or cold drafts, insufficient fertilizer, and a potbound root system.

Disorder	*Possible causes*
BUDS FAIL TO OPEN, WITHER OR DROP OFF	Insufficient light Air too dry Overwatering

PETAL & LEAF TIPS TURN BROWN	Check soil:
	    if DRY, water more often or more thoroughly
	    if MOIST, cause may be high salts: LEACH soil
	Air too dry

LEAVES TURN YELLOW OR BROWN	Check soil:
	    if DRY, water more often or more thoroughly
	    if MOIST, cause may be high salts: LEACH soil
	    if WET, may be poor drainage or simply overwatering
	Temperature too high
	Air too dry
	Insufficient fresh air

BROWN SPOTS ON PETALS & LEAVES	Overwatering or poor drainage Light too bright
FLOWERS & LEAVES CURL UP	Hot or cold draft Aphids
FLOWERS & LEAVES FALL OFF	Overwatering or poor drainage Insufficient light Soil very dry Cold draft Injury caused by manufactured gas
LEAVES PALE GREEN OR YELLOW	Too little or too much light Plant needs fertilizer Temperature too high
NEW GROWTH THIN AND PALE	Too little light Too much nitrogen (N) in fertilizer Temperature too high
LEAVES ARE PALE OR YELLOW WITH GREEN VEINS	Plant needs fertilizer pH too high (iron unavailable): Water at normal times with solution of 2 tsp. lemon juice in 1 pt. water.
NEW LEAVES SMALL	Plant needs repotting—check roots Plant needs fertilizer Injury caused by high salts: LEACH soil Temperature too high

PLANT WILTS	Check soil:
	    if DRY, water more often or more thoroughly
	    if MOIST, cause may be high salts: LEACH soil
	    if WET, may be poor drainage or simply overwatering
	Plant needs repotting—check roots
	Air too dry

WHOLE PLANT SUDDENLY COLLAPSES	Roots dead, caused by water saturation and/or high salts Cold or hot draft
GROWTH STUNTED	Roots dying, caused by water saturation and/or high salts
ROOTS APPEAR ON SOIL SURFACE	Roots may be waterlogged or completely dry in lower part of container Plant needs repotting—check roots
PLANT ROTS AT OR JUST ABOVE SOIL LEVEL	Too much water, caused by overwatering or poor drainage Too cold

To LEACH: see Soluble Salts and Leaching, page 6

Common Name Index

Common Name Index Continued

Mapleleaf Begonia *(Begonia x 'Cleopatra')* 21
Miniature Pouch Flower *(Hypocyrta wettsteinii)* 46
Miniature Rose *(Rosa chinensis hybrida)* 71
Miniature Sinningia *(Sinningia species)* 49
Miniature Slipper Plant *(Sinningia concinna)* 49
Miniature Slipper Plant *(Sinningia pusilla)* 49
Miniature Spathiphyllum *(Spathiphyllum floribundum)* 15
Miniature Wandering Jew *(Gibasis geniculata)* 51
Moon Valley Pilea *(Pilea 'Moon Valley')* 64
Mother of Thousands *(Saxifraga sarmentosa)* 66
Mum Plant *(Chrysanthemum morifolium)* 36, 37

Oilcloth Flower *(Anthurium andraeanum)* 14
Orange Star *(Guzmania lingulata 'Minor')* 26
Orchid *(see Cattleya, Paphiopedilum)*
Ornamental Pepper *(Capsicum species)* 34

Panamiga *(Pilea involucrata)* 64
Painted Nettle *(Coleus blumei)* 31
Pansy Geranium *(Pelargonium x domesticum)* 62
Parlor Ivy *(Senecio mikanioides)* 66
Patience *(Impatiens walleriana sultani)* 54
Patient Lucy *(Impatiens walleriana sultani)* 54
Peace Lily *(Spathiphyllum 'Clevelandii')* 15
Pendulous Begonia *(Begonia tuberhybrida)* 23
Persian Violet *(Exacum affine)* 42
Pin Cushion *(Mammillaria hybrid)* 28
Pink Brocade *(Episcia 'Pink Brocade')* 47
Pink Florida Christ-Thorn *(Euphorbia x 'Flamingo')* 29
Pocketbook Plant *(Calceolaria herbeohybrida)* 32
Poinsettia *(Euphorbia pulcherrima)* 68, 69
Polyantha Rose *(Rosa x polyantha)* 71
Polyanthus Primrose *(Primula x polyantha)* 70
Pot Chrysanthemum *(Chrysanthemum morifolium)* 36, 37
Prostrate Coleus *(Plectranthus oertendahlii)* 65

Queen of Orchids *(Cattleya hybrid)* 60, 61
Queen's Tears *(Billbergia nutans)* 25

Rainbow Cactus *(Echinocereus pectinatus v. neomexicanus)* 28
Red Cluster Pepper *(Capsicum annuum 'Fiesta'* 34
Red Hot Cat-Tail *(Acalypha hispida)* 10
Regal Geranium *(Pelargonium x domesticum)* 62
Rose Geranium *(Pelargonium graveolens)* 62
Rose Heath *(Erica gracilis)* 41
Roving Soldier *(Saxifraga sarmentosa)*

Saffron Spike Zebra *(Aphelandra squarrosa)* 11
Scented Geranium *(Pelargonium graveolens)* 62
Scented Leaf Geranium *(Pelargonium graveolens)* 62
Shamrock *(Oxalis rubra alba)* 67
Show Geranium *(Pelargonium x domesticum)* 62
Shrimp Plant *(Beloperone guttata)* 10
Shrub Verbena *(Lantana camara)* 59
Silver Vase *(Aechmea fasciata)* 24
Snowball Plant *(Hydrangea macrophylla)* 53
Spathe Flower *(Spathiphyllum floribundum)* 15
Spotted Flowering Maple *(Abutilon striatum thompsonii)* 9
Spurflower *(Plectranthus oertendahlii)* 65
Strawberry Begonia *(Saxifraga sarmentosa)* 66
Strawberry Geranium *(Saxifraga sarmentosa)* 66
Sultana Impatiens *(Impatiens wallerian sultani)* 54

Tabasco Pepper *(Capsicum annuum conoides)* 34
Tahitian Bridal Veil *(Gibasis geniculata)* 51
Tailflower *(Anthurium andraeanum)* 14
Thanksgiving Cactus *(Zygocactus truncatus)* 30
Touch-Me-Not *(Impatiens walleriana sultani)* 54
Tropicana Pouch Flower *(Hypocyrta 'tropicana')* 46
Troutleaf Begonia *(Begonia 'Medora')* 19
Tuberous Begonia *(Begonia tuberhybrida)* 23

Usambara *(Saintpaulia ionantha)* 48

Variegated Wax Begonia *(Begonia semperflorens 'Charm')* 22
Vase Plant *(Aechmea calyculata)* 24
Velvet Swedish Ivy *(Plectranthus oertendahlii)* 65
Violet Slipper Gloxinia *(Sinningia speciosa)* 50

Water Ivy *(Senecio mikanioides)* 66
Wax Begonia *(Begonia semperflorens)* 22
Wax Plant *(Hoya minata)* 52
Weeping Chinese Lantern *(Abutilon megapotamicum variegatum)* 9
White Anthurium *(Sapthiphyllum 'Clevelandii')* 15
White Flag *(Spathiphyllum 'Clevelandii')* 15
Window Box Oxalis *(Oxalis rubra alba)* 67

Zebra Plant *(Aphelandra squarrosa)* 11
Zonal Geranium *(Pelargonium x hortorum)* 63

Botanical Name Index

Botanical Name Index Continued